Original title:
Tropical Delights

Copyright © 2025 Creative Arts Management OÜ
All rights reserved.

Author: Eleanor Prescott
ISBN HARDBACK: 978-1-80581-635-5
ISBN PAPERBACK: 978-1-80581-162-6
ISBN EBOOK: 978-1-80581-635-5

Rhythm of the Tides

The waves dance with a silly grin,
Crabs do the cha-cha, let the fun begin!
Seagulls squawk, they're quite the jest,
Surfboards tumble, who rides the best?

Flip-flops fly from feet with style,
Sandy shorts, the latest in aisle!
Ocean's giggle, a splash of cheer,
Catch a wave, hold on, oh dear!

Beneath the Banyan

Under the branches, critters play,
Monkeys swing, they shout hooray!
Lizards lounge with a sunbaked frown,
While ants parade in a tiny crown.

The breeze whispers, 'What's the scoop?'
As squirrels gather for a nutty troop!
Picnic mishaps, all in good fun,
Beneath the tree, we've just begun!

Liquid Sunshine

Mango smoothies in a blender whirl,
Pineapple sips cause a tropical twirl!
Coconut laughter in every glass,
Tasting joy, such a merry class.

Ice cream sundaes melt on a plate,
With sprinkles galore, oh, isn't it great!
Sip a toast with a goofy cheer,
To liquid sunshine, we hold dear!

Spice Route Reverie

Saffron dreams in a curry stew,
Chili's kick makes everyone woo!
A dash of humor in each bite,
Spices dancing, what a delight!

Ginger jokes, they tickle the tongue,
While nutmeg stories are often sung.
Taste buds giggle with every chew,
On the spice route, we find our crew!

Colors of the Coral

Splashes of pink and bright green,
The fish swim by, not quite seen.
A clownfish tries to steal the show,
But it's the seaweed that's stealing the glow.

Bubble-blowing is an art,
The starfish just won't play its part.
Anemones dance with a cheeky grin,
While crabs throw parties we can't begin.

Sunkissed Tides

The sunbeams tickle the ocean's face,
While seagulls squawk in a clumsy race.
Shells hide secrets, a mystery steep,
But don't ask the hermit, he's lost in sleep.

Surfboards tumble like beachball clowns,
As laughter echoes and joy abounds.
Sandcastles wobble, soon to collapse,
Built by hands with all the mishaps.

Rhythms of the Shore

Breezes whistle a light-hearted tune,
As crabs jive under the sunny moon.
Dancing waves wear a foamy dress,
While the wind shouts, 'You must confess!'

Seashells drumbeat on the shore,
A pelican lands, what a score!
Tide pools giggle with a splash,
As starfish attempt a belly flop crash.

Twilight in the Tropics

Colors fade with a playful wink,
As monkeys swing from the palm tree's brink.
The sunset's palette, an artist's dream,
While mosquitoes plot, oh how they scheme!

Laughter echoes through the leaves,
Where everyone shares their funny heaves.
As night falls down like a fluffy sock,
The beach becomes a comedy rock.

Raindrop Reverie

The raindrops dance on the coconut tree,
Laughing as they tickle the bumblebee.
Splashing in puddles, a raucous cheer,
They whisper secrets that only we hear.

A parrot squawks, wearing a silly hat,
While a crab does the cha-cha; oh, imagine that!
Coconuts roll like they're in a race,
Nature's own circus, a comical place.

Secrets of the Lagoon

In the lagoon, the fish gossip galore,
About the old turtle who dreams of the shore.
They flash their scales in a playful show,
As a gecko stirs up a jellyfish woe.

The lily pads giggle beneath the sun,
While frogs croak jokes; oh, what fun!
A water snake slips with a wink of an eye,
As it plots a prank on the dragonfly.

Essence of Sunlight

The sun peeks through like a jolly old friend,
Chasing the shadows, a lively trend.
A beach ball rolls with a giggly sound,
Knocking over flip-flops lying around.

The rays sprinkle laughter on sandy toes,
Running in circles as the warm wind blows.
Ice cream cones wobble and sway with glee,
As seagulls swoop down for their share of free.

Laughter of the Lagoon

The lagoon is alive with a croaking choir,
Each note a ripple, a joke to inspire.
A turtle tumbles, it's laughing so hard,
While fish play tag, not a moment's a guard.

Bananas swing from the palm tree's embrace,
As the monkeys tumble in a runaway race.
Under the water, a crab holds a show,
With a dance that would make even mermaids go
"Whoa!"

Fuchsia Fantasies

In a land of pink lemonade,
Where pineapples wear tiny hats,
The iguanas dance in shades,
While sipping tea with chitchat.

The coconuts start a band,
Playing tunes of sweet delight,
With papayas taking lead,
And the mangoes dancing bright.

Who knew a parrot could sing,
While twirling on a branch so high?
The sun just grinned, it's a fling,
As rainbow ice cream drops from the sky!

So join the jubilee parade,
With fruit hats and silly shoes,
In fuchsia dreams, we serenade,
And laugh until we snooze.

Oasis of Dreams

In a splash of lagoons so blue,
Where the lizards wear sunglasses cool,
Watermelons float and queue,
For a dive in the silly pool.

A camel juggles juicy dates,
While pineapples don't lose their zest,
There's laughter on the dinner plates,
As marshmallow clouds build a nest.

Everyone's dancing with glee,
As the wind plays tunes from afar,
With iguanas tapping their feet,
Underneath the candy star.

So come, enjoy this charming spree,
Where even sunsets chuckle and spin,
In the oasis where we all agree,
That laughter is where fun begins!

Echoes of Seashells

In the sand, I found a shell,
Hope it whispers tales to tell.
But it just shouts, 'Who's my friend?'
I laugh and wonder where it ends.

A crab walks by, strikes a pose,
With tiny legs and a funny nose.
I clap for him, he winks at me,
We dance along the glistening sea.

Cloudless Horizons

The sky is blue, the sun's a clown,
It laughs and beams, then falls right down.
I caught it once, it slipped away,
Now it hides for the rest of the day.

A parrot sings in colors bright,
With jokes that make the dolphins bite.
They giggle and splash in their watery show,
While I just sit, and enjoy the flow.

Paradise in Petals

Flowers bloom, and bees just hum,
They buzz around, a lively drum.
One bee stopped, said, 'What's the buzz?'
I told it jokes, it laughed because!

A lizard steals my sun hat,
He thinks he's cool, he really's not.
With shades on, he tries to groove,
But tripping roots make him lose his move.

Festival of Colors

Painted skies and dancing lights,
Fish in flip-flops join the sights.
I asked a goldfish for some scoops,
He gave me glances, but no loops!

A monkey throws confetti high,
Says, 'Catch it quick, or watch me fly!'
With laughter from the branches near,
We toast to fun, and sip our cheer.

Pina Colada Dreams

A blender spins in merry dance,
With coconut, and rum's romance.
Pineapple chunks joyfully fly,
As I sip and watch the sky!

The ice cubes clink like silver chimes,
While I invent some wacky rhymes.
A straw gets tangled in my hair,
I laugh and wonder if I care!

The drink is gone, my head's a whirl,
I dream of beaches and a girl.

Seafoam Secrets

Waves crash down with playful cheer,
Whispers of laughter, can you hear?
Seagulls giggle, on the prowl,
As I dodge their next food foul.

Flip-flops flying off my feet,
Chasing crabs, oh what a feat!
Sandcastle towers, oh so grand,
Only to fall at my command.

Balloons drift up, I let them go,
They dance above in splendid show.
With salty kisses on my face,
I twirl around in this wild space.

Garden of Serenity

Flowers bloom in colors bright,
Buzzing bees, what pure delight!
A timer set for playful pranks,
As I sneak up on the rank.

Ladybugs with tiny shields,
Help me conquer grassy fields.
In this paradise of bloom,
I giggle at a dandelion's plume.

The sun dips low, I chase the light,
Trip on vines, an epic sight!
With petals stuck upon my nose,
I laugh until the evening goes.

Swaying Silhouettes

Palm trees sway like disco queens,
Inviting all to join their scenes.
I dance like no one's watching me,
While shadows laugh, oh what glee!

Bikini straps take off like tights,
As I dive into neon nights.
Friends spin 'round in hula twirls,
With silly grins and ocean swirls.

The beach ball bounces just for fun,
A game of catch, oh what a run!
With laughter echoing through the day,
I sway and twirl my cares away.

Mirage of Melodies

Beneath the sun, a hammock sways,
A parrot sings in funny ways.
The coconut drops, it's quite a sight,
Napping sunscreens left in plight.

A monkey steals the fruity snacks,
While folks just giggle, hum, and quack.
The waves roll in like silly clowns,
As flip-flops dance on sandy grounds.

Nectar of the Tropics

In colors bright, the drinks await,
With straws like snakes that love to date.
A lime twist here, a splash of fun,
Wait, was that drink? Or was it sun?

Belly laughs from beachy folk,
Slipping on waves, it's quite the joke.
Pineapples wear sarongs with flair,
As coconuts giggle without a care.

Dancers in the Heat

Beneath the palm, the dancers glide,
With hula hoops that twist and slide.
The sun plays tricks, it hides then peeks,
And coconut shells hide awkward squeaks.

The beach ball bounces, a round affair,
While sandcastles lose their hair.
Goofy moves abound this scene,
As flip-flops turn into tambourines.

Paradise Found

A treasure hunt with spoons and forks,
In sandy pits where laughter storks.
The sunburned noses all in rows,
Are signaling that fun just grows.

Seagulls squawk like they know best,
While beach towels take a cozy rest.
In this haven of sun-kissed bliss,
Even the sunscreen hopes for a kiss.

Island Whispers

On the shore where coconuts fall,
A crab ordered a drink, not small.
   He sipped with such flair,
   Said, "Life's but a dare!"

The sun wore shades, quite absurd,
While parrots gossip in a word.
   "Did you see that last dive?"
   "Oh, what a jive!"

A turtle in flip-flops strolled by,
Left sand castles, oh my, oh my!
   "Just looking for shade,
   In this grand parade!"

A piña colada's the drink of choice,
While the sea breezes cheerfully voice:
   "To laughter and fun,
   Let's dance in the sun!"

Sun-Kissed Reflections

A sunbeam slipped on a banana peel,
And landed on a fish with zeal.
They laughed and they danced,
In this world entranced.

A seagull sang a tune so sweet,
Claimed he invented the beach retreat!
With sunglasses on,
He held court till dawn.

The sandcastles all had grand dreams,
Of water slides and chocolate streams.
But when waves would crash,
Their hopes turned to ash.

Under stars where the coconuts sway,
The night giggles in its play.
With laughter so light,
They danced till daylight.

Lush Paradise Secrets

In a garden where the pineapples joke,
A mango tried to be a bad folk.
"I'm ripe and I'm round,
But lost and unfound!"

The kiwi was wearing a polka dot hat,
Said, "Join us for tea, but not with a cat!"
They giggled and swayed,
In their fruit masquerade.

Palm trees swayed to a maraca's beat,
While a squirrel tap danced with its feet.
"Let's party all night,
In this shimmering light!"

The breeze whispered tales to the moon,
While frogs croaked a comical tune.
With laughter on breeze,
Frogs lounged with ease!

Mango Dreams at Dusk

As the sun dipped low with a wink,
A mango fell off, quick as a blink.
"I'm ripe, I'm fine,
Let's party and dine!"

The moon peeked out, gave a cheer,
While a pineapple conquered his fear.
Said, "I'll dance tonight,
With fruit, oh what a sight!"

The dance floor shined with a glow,
As the limes rolled in with a show.
"Let's twist and we'll shout,
Make the world spin about!"

Under stars where all flavors collide,
The fruits laughed together with pride.
In dreams draped in dusk,
Their giggles a must!

The Sway of Coconut Palms

Coconuts drop with a thud,
Watch out, folks, here comes the flood!
Palm trees dancing in the breeze,
Look out for snacks, they're sure to please.

Monkeys swing on branches high,
Chasing crabs and birds that fly.
Sipping juice from a bright green shell,
Feeling dazed? Just ring the bell!

Sun-kissed laughter fills the air,
Flip-flops flying without a care.
The hammock sways like a boat,
Don't fall off! It's a slippery moat.

Underneath the palm trees' sway,
We'll dance like no one's led astray.
With every wave, our giggles blend,
Till sunset, let the good times extend!

Seashell Serenade

A seashell whispers on the shore,
"Pick me up! I'm never a bore!"
Waves crash in, a hearty cheer,
A crab joins in, oh dear, oh dear!

The seagulls cackle, they've got style,
Surfboards slipping, just for a while.
Sandy tunes and laughter rise,
Don't mind the fish; it's all a surprise!

The golden sun starts to dip low,
A clam-shaped boat begins to glow.
With cocktails made of bright sea foam,
In this beach bliss, we find our home.

A conch shell sings, "Please stay awhile,"
As dolphins dance and sea stars smile.
Let's make memories by the score,
With seashells trotting on the shore!

Dancing with Hibiscus

Hibiscus blooms in hues so bright,
They twirl in gardens, pure delight.
Butterflies flutter, putting on a show,
Dancing with blooms, they steal the glow.

A bee bumbles, searching for treats,
He trips and tumbles on soft, warm seats.
Petals giggle in the warm sun's bath,
Join the dance, come share the path!

The breeze carries perfume so sweet,
With every stomp, we're on our feet.
Swaying wildly in a floral craze,
Laughter echoes, it's a joyous maze!

Under the moon, we'll waltz and spin,
With every blush, the night begins.
A garden party with funky flair,
Hibiscus friends, we'll dance with care!

Coral Reef Symphony

Under the waves, a concert lives,
Fish and seaweed play, oh what a sieve!
Turtles tap dance with flair and grace,
Join the fun in this underwater space.

Clownfish jest in colors ablaze,
Tickling shrimp in coral's gaze.
The sea anemone sways to the beat,
While starfish wiggle their groovy feet.

An octopus juggles shells with ease,
Creating smiles, invoking 'oohs' and 'fees'.
Every creature takes their turn,
In this show, there's plenty to learn!

As the sun beams down, a beckoning ray,
We flip and flop, in a silly ballet.
With giggles and splashes, our hearts take flight,
In this coral symphony, joy feels just right!

Twilight Blossoms

Sunset skies in colors bright,
Dancing flowers in the light.
Bees in tutus buzzing near,
Whispering secrets, bright and clear.

Frogs in masks hold evening shows,
Jumping high in silly poses.
Fireflies twinkle like a star,
Pineapple hats—what a bizarre!

Ladybugs with tiny dreams,
Sipping nectar, plotting schemes.
While the world just laughs and spins,
Nature's folly, where joy begins.

Shadows of Coconut Trees

Under palms, the shadows play,
Squirrels host their nut parade.
Coconuts roll with a thud,
As monkeys giggle, oh what a dud!

Crabs with shades, they strut along,
Singing loudly an off-key song.
The sun's still up, but they won't care,
Jiving lightly without a scare.

Breezes whisper silly jokes,
As sea turtles share their pokes.
Coconut water on the rocks,
Who knew life could be such a hoax?

Ocean Embrace

Waves that tickle sandy toes,
Seagulls wear their fancy clothes.
Surfers dance on foam so white,
While fishes giggle, what a sight!

A crab is dressed in polka dots,
Drinking soda from a pot.
Mermaids laugh in glee, oh my!
As dolphins leap beneath the sky.

Sand castles built with silly flair,
The king is just a teddy bear.
Shells that sing a wandering tune,
Here, every wave is a cartoon.

Dune Dancer's Tale

In the dunes, the lizards prance,
Chasing shadows, doing the dance.
Tumbleweeds roll by with glee,
Who knew the desert had esprit?

Cacti wear their funny hats,
While rabbits gossip with the brats.
Winds that tickle, sand that flies,
A sunburned camel rolls his eyes.

Kites that argue in the breeze,
Flicking about like hyper bees.
Every day's a tale to tell,
In the dunes, where laughter dwells.

Melodies in the Mist

A monkey misplaces his hat,
Sings to the parrot, 'Where's my mat?'
They laugh and they dance on the breeze,
While the iguanas just snack on some peas.

Coconuts roll down the hill,
One lands on a snail as he chills.
The waves clap their hands in delight,
As the sun sets, painting the night.

A crab moonwalks, what a sight!
While a pelican takes a flight.
Everyone joins in the fun,
Chasing shadows till day is done.

With a splash and a flurry of cheer,
The laughter of friends you can hear.
In this paradise, joy is the quest,
Every moment, simply the best.

Essence of the Waterfall

The waterfall giggles and splashes,
As fish put on their finny stashes.
A frog tries to jump with style,
Lands in a pool—it's all worth the while.

Bamboo sways like a dancer bright,
While the breeze puts on a playful fight.
A turtle slow-mo struts along,
Humming the island's silly song.

Butterflies flutter, don't hold your breath,
As they chase each other to a near-death.
A snail complains, "I'm late as can be!"
While a crab laughs, "Just hurry to see!"

Water splashes, a jaguar grins,
As nature giggles; joy always wins.
In this wild world, where folly reigns,
Every drop soaks up the playful gains.

Colors of a Sunlit Day

Bright parrots critique the sunrise hue,
'Is it orange or yellow? Who knew!'
While flamingos try to find their pose,
Landing on one leg through the rose.

A pineapple rolls down the steep shore,
While a turtle shouts, "I can't take much more!"
The coconuts practice their jokes,
Strutting and giggling like playful folks.

A sandcastle stands—a wobbly tower,
While the tide grins with its salty power.
Children run, dodging waves with glee,
As their laughter joins the ocean's spree.

The sun dips low, casting shadows wide,
As the day waves goodbye with pride.
In this land where colors collide,
Joy and fun forever reside.

Heartbeat of the Island

A toucan beeps with a silly cheer,
As the rhythm of laughter draws near.
Bamboo sticks play the calypso tune,
As a crab shakes it under the moon.

The turtles form a dance-off line,
While the shrimp jive, looking divine.
A goat wears sunglasses, what a sight!
While the waves crash with all their might.

Glimpses of paradise everywhere,
With a pinch of chaos in the air.
Each creature unique, fun in their way,
Crafting memories day by day.

As the sun sets over the bay,
The island smiles, come what may.
In this heartbeat, laughter is found,
Uniting all in a joy-filled sound.

Palette of Paradise

In a land where pineapples giggle,
Coconuts dance with a comical wiggle,
Mangoes play tag with the cheerful sun,
The fruit salad sings, oh what fun!

Lemons wear shades, they're quite the sight,
Watermelons chuckle in pure delight,
Bananas slip on their peel with a grin,
Each quirky fruit invites you in.

Berry-Blossom Dreams

Blueberries burst like balloons in the night,
Raspberries wear crowns, they feel so bright,
Strawberries strut with a berry-leaf flair,
While blackberries giggle, swinging in air.

Peaches gossip from their fluffy throne,
Cherries bounce around, never alone,
Fruit salad parties on a sunny beam,
Every bite's sweeter than any dream.

Driftwood Dialogues

Driftwood winks as the ocean hums,
Shells are dancing like playful drums,
A crab tells tales of the tide's great fuss,
While seagulls squabble with a laugh and a fuss.

The sand giggles as kids jump high,
Building castles with dreams that touch the sky,
The sun tosses ribbons of golden rays,
While nature chuckles through endless days.

Sunset on Golden Sands

As the sun dips low, it paints the sky,
Fluffy clouds blush, oh me, oh my!
A beach ball rolls with a silly thud,
While flip-flops leave behind a playful mud.

Seashells whisper secrets in a jive,
The tide pulls back like it's brought to life,
With laughter echoing through the evening breeze,
Nature shares jokes like the tallest trees.

Echoes of Paradise

In the sun, the coconuts sway,
Mangoes giggle, they want to play.
Crabs in shorts, doing the cha-cha,
While a parrot shouts, 'Hasta la vista!'

Flip-flops clapping on sandy toes,
As a pineapple yodels, the party grows.
Seagulls are dancing, what a sight!
While tourists juggle, oh what a fright!

Ferns and Feathers

Ferns wiggle like they've got a beat,
While toucans strut on vibrant feet.
Monkeys chuckle, swinging by,
At a tree house bar, they aim to try.

Lizards laugh, racing down the vine,
Wearing tiny hats and sipping brine.
Their funny faces make us grin,
What a wild party, let's dive in!

Saltwater Auras

Ocean waves splash, a playful tease,
Fish in sunglasses swim with ease.
A starfish crawls, waving with flair,
While dolphins squirt water in the air.

Beach balls bouncing, kids take flight,
Sandy castles, a comical sight.
Seashells giggle in the sun's warm light,
Chasing crabs while sipping sprite!

Vibrant Nights

Under the moon, the rhythms ignite,
Fireflies twinkle, a spectacular sight.
Dancers spin, their shadows play,
As laughter echoes, night turns to day.

Karaoke night with a twist of lime,
A coconut serenading in rhyme.
Everyone's laughing, feeling so free,
Even a palm tree joins in the spree!

The Sway of Coconuts

In the breeze, they dance and twirl,
A coconut falls, oh boy, what a swirl!
Monkeys giggle high in the trees,
Throwing down nuts with such gentle ease.

Watch out, here comes a cheeky bird,
Pecking at shells, it's absurd!
With each loud thud, we grin and laugh,
Coconuts might just be our gaffe.

Sip that juice, it's a funny sight,
Best served cold on a sunny night.
Parrots squawking, they join the spree,
Their chatter's as wild as we can be.

In the warmth, our worries flee,
Underneath that palm tree spree.
With coconuts raining down like snow,
We'll dance till the sun says hello!

Sunkissed Serenade

Oh the sun, how it loves to play,
Painting smiles in a golden display.
We skip along the sandy shore,
Singing songs, oh what's in store?

A seagull struts, quite out of tune,
Dancing around like a cartoon.
Shells giggle as we step on by,
In this silly world, we're all awry!

The waves come splashing with a shout,
Tickling toes, without a doubt.
Seaweed wigs on our heads we wear,
Laughing so hard, without a care.

As the sun dips low and skies ignite,
Our shadows stretch, a silly sight.
In this moment, life's truly grand,
Sunkissed fun in this sunny land!

Secrets of the Coral Reef

Beneath the waves, fish giggle in glee,
A clownfish grins, as bright as can be.
A turtle swims, so slow and chill,
What secrets it keeps, it's quite the thrill!

Coral castles have tales to tell,
Of dolphins who dance and jellyfish swell.
With fins that flap, they swirl around,
Creating a party without a sound!

An octopus winks with eight arms wide,
Playing peek-a-boo, oh what a ride!
With ink that squirts under the sea,
They all laugh because they're so free.

The reef is a world of unseen delight,
Where starfish laugh, twinkling bright.
In this watery realm, we lose our pride,
Secrets abound, let's take a dive!

Lullaby of the Ocean

The ocean hums a gentle tune,
As evening falls beneath the moon.
Waves come crashing, soft and low,
Rocking us like a sweetened show.

A crab crawls sideways with a groove,
Its silly dance makes us move!
Starfish clapping on the sand,
Joining in, giving a hand.

The moonlight sparkles on the sea,
As fish swim by, making us glee.
In the distance, a boat does sway,
With laughter echoing far away.

Close your eyes, let dreams take flight,
As the ocean sings goodnight.
A lullaby of joy and cheer,
In this watery world, there's nothing to fear!

Rhythm of Raindrops

Pitter-patter on the roof,
Splish-splash, what a goof!
Dancing puddles, here they come,
With a splash and a thump.

Drip-drop, frogs say hello,
Jumping high, putting on a show.
Umbrellas spin, hats fly far,
As we dodge the raindrop star!

Water's everywhere, oh dear!
Laughing friends all dance in cheer.
Slipping slides and squeals abound,
Round and round, we spin around!

Raindrops playing tricks on me,
Wetting socks, oh, so carefree!
In this dance, we laugh and glide,
Hiding from the raindrop slide!

Harvest of the Sun

Sunny skies, and a grin so wide,
Melons rolling, we all decide.
Catch them quick, it's like a game,
Squeezing juice, what a fame!

Mango madness, sticky hands,
Grinning while taste testing bands.
Banana peels, oh what a slip,
In the sun, we all just rip!

Pineapples in a juicy fight,
With each bite, we take flight.
Lemonade stands spring up fast,
But we chug and cheer, unsurpassed!

Sun-kissed faces, waves of fun,
Harvest laughter, oh what a run.
As we play in fields of gold,
Funny tales of joy unfold!

Canvas of Hibiscus

Colors bright in gardens sway,
Hibiscus blooms come out to play.
Painting petals, reds and pinks,
Such beauty makes us laugh and wink.

Buzzing bees on a wild spree,
Dancing 'round, oh can't you see?
With each flower, a tale is spun,
Life's canvas is never done!

Little bugs hold fancy feasts,
In this garden, laughter's yeast.
Pollen darts like little darts,
Creating joy in little hearts!

Hibiscus hats, funny and grand,
Wear them now, show off your hand.
In the garden, singing loudly,
Nature's giggles bounce so proudly!

Sunlit Harbour

Boats a-bobbing, sun shines bright,
Seagulls squawking in sheer delight.
Fishing lines tangled, what a sight,
Reeling in jokes, oh what a bite!

Beach balls bouncing, laughter flows,
Building castles, everyone knows.
Sandy toes and salty tricks,
Ice cream cones, with funny licks!

Chasing crabs who dart away,
Snap, snap, giggling, they're at play.
With each wave, a squeal is heard,
Surfboard slips, oh how absurd!

Sunlit harbour, vibrant and warm,
With every splash, we find our charm.
Laughter echoes, here we stay,
In this joyful, sunlit bay!

Vibrant Petal Dance

In a garden where colors clash,
Petals shimmy, oh what a splash!
A flower tried to do the twist,
And lost its head, oh what a lisp!

Bees buzzed in a conga line,
But tripped on pollen, feeling fine.
They laughed and fell, what a silly sight,
Waltzing in blooms, lost to the night.

A butterfly lost its sense of flair,
Tangled up in a ladybug's hair.
They laughed so hard, they danced on the breeze,
Creating jigs among the trees.

In this garden of jolly and cheer,
Even the grasshoppers joined in the beer.
They tapped their feet, and took a chance,
In the vibrant petal dance!

Coral Reflections

Fish in tuxedos, swimming in style,
Doing the cha-cha along the aisle.
A crab in a top hat, looking quite grand,
Lost his way while holding a hand!

Starfish twirled with a clumsy grace,
Said, "Look at me, I'm getting my space!"
But slipped on some kelp, oh what a mess,
Now in a conga line, feeling blessed!

An octopus juggled pearls with a frown,
While the clownfish giggled, swimming around.
"Hey, can you share?" they called out in glee,
"We'd love to join your talent spree!"

Under the waves, the laughter spread,
As jellyfish floated, feeling quite red.
Coral reefs echoed with joyous vibes,
Where silliness thrived, along with the jibes!

A Symphony of Mangoes

Mangoes burst with giggles and grins,
Rolling around in fruit-filled bins.
One tried to dance, but took a slide,
Ended up stuck, oh what a ride!

A coconut cracked jokes from the tree,
While the papayas sang harmony.
Together they formed a silly band,
Juicy fruit music, oh so grand!

Bananas slipped, then took a spin,
Banana peels made laughter begin.
Kiwis joined in, with zest and cheer,
Playing tambourines, spreading good cheer!

The kitchen turned into a fruity spree,
As smoothies giggled with glee.
A symphony born from sunshine bright,
Making fruit salad through the night!

Twilight in Paradise

Sunset paints the sky in shades,
While crickets start their merry parades.
A toucan sipping juice, feeling fine,
Must have had too much, oh what a line!

Palm trees wiggled with delight,
As the stars came out, twinkles so bright.
A bet between monkeys, swinging afar,
Who could throw coconuts the farthest star!

The ocean giggled, waves crashed playfully,
Even the seashells joined the jubilee.
A starfish wearing shades stole the show,
Saying, "Life is better when you just let go!"

In this twilight where mischief reigns,
We danced with the sunset, embracing the gains.
Laughter echoed from beach to shore,
In paradise moments, who could ask for more?

Sun-Kissed Shores

On sun-kissed sands, a crab took a stroll,
In flip-flops worn by a beach ball's roll.
Seagulls gossip, their tales quite absurd,
While sunbathers snore, missing every word.

A coconut dropped, what a chaotic scene,
Bystanders laughed, was it a prank or a dream?
The tide rolled in, stealing snacks on parade,
And sandy sandwiches were all that they made.

Laughter erupted from waves crashing near,
As a buoy-turned-floaty became their dear sphere.
Playing hide and seek with crabs on a spree,
While sunset melted like warm, gooey brie.

And as night dawned, with stars up above,
The beach was alive, sealed with heartfelt love.
With sand in their toes, they'd dance and they'd cheer,
Making memories, oh, how the fun would steer!

Lush Canopy Dreams

In the jungle thick, where vines twist and twine,
A monkey named Lou found a hat with a shine.
He wore it with pride, a fashion so rare,
Swinging through branches with flair, beyond compare!

Parrots squawked jokes, painting trees bright as day,
As toucans laughed loud in their comical play.
The sloth joined the fun, though very, very slow,
Saying, "I'll arrive... just you wait, don't you go!"

Beneath leafy shades, a picnic was spread,
Bananas in smoothies, while chattering fled.
A surprise insect dance on a platter so fine,
Made all of them giggle while sipping on brine.

The canopy echoed with humor so sweet,
In a world of fun where no one faced defeat.
With giggles and chatter amidst laughter's throng,
The jungle sang praises, a whimsical song!

Fragrant Breeze

In a garden bright, where flowers come alive,
A bee made a joke that could truly contrive.
"Why do petals blush?" it buzzed with delight,
"Because they get tickled by sunlight at night!"

The breezes laughed back, carrying sweet tunes,
As daisies chimed in, beneath bright, playful moons.
Lavender chuckled with aromas so wise,
As butterflies danced beneath painted skies.

A snail in a race wore a cap made of leaves,
Said, "Wait till the end; you'll see how I weave!"
While crickets composed symphonies loud,
They formed a small band, gathering a crowd!

In this fragrant realm, where whimsies arise,
Each flutter and chuckle brought joy to the skies.
With scents swirling forth like a playful cheer,
The garden giggled, making all worries disappear!

Island Memoirs

On an island bright where the coconuts sway,
A parrot named Pete caused quite the dismay.
He mimicked the sound of a very loud sneeze,
And everyone there just fell down to their knees!

A crab with some sass strutted with style,
Claiming his patch, he could conquer a mile.
A flip-flop flew past, all haughty and proud,
As the hermit crabs shouted, "Join in, don't crowd!"

While locals played games with some coconut balls,
Laughter erupted and echoed through halls.
A contest ensued for the best dance move,
And the winner was truly a weird little groove.

As sunset approached, stories started to spin,
Of quests near the shore, and the wild tales within.
With smiles all around, and shadows so long,
These island memoirs forever would throng!

Nectar of the Rainforest

In the jungle, fruits so bright,
Monkeys swing, what a sight!
A pineapple wears a crown,
While coconut drinks it down.

Parrots squawk, their colors clash,
While sloths move with a slow smash.
Bees buzz near a flower's face,
Wishing honey was their base.

Gorillas groove to jungle tunes,
As they eat those leafy spoons.
Swaying vines, a dance so grand,
Who knew plants could be so bland?

With each bite, a silly grin,
Fruit salad fun, let the feast begin!
Laughter rolls through sunlit glades,
Nature sings, it's time for parades.

Hidden Oasis

In the sands, a splash, a splash,
Palm trees sway with a sunny bash.
A camel struts in shades of brown,
While flip-flops flop, all over town.

Fruity drinks in coconuts,
Next to a pig that loudly struts.
Sunburned tourists wear a frown,
As the ice cream cones fall down.

A sunbather tries to tan,
Gets chased away by a tiny man.
With more sunscreen than in a shop,
Hoping he won't ever flop.

Frolicking kids in water sprays,
Giggling under sun's warm rays.
In this paradise, joy is loud,
As laughter gathers quite the crowd.

Chasing the Horizon

On a boat with a silly crew,
Mixing drinks, oh what a view!
The ocean winks, a playful tease,
As seagulls cackle in the breeze.

With surfboards shaped like giant fish,
They ride the waves, and oh, what a wish!
To catch a wave without a splash,
But end up with a massive crash.

Sailing sunsets, colors clash,
Navigating love with a splash.
A mermaid surfaces with a grin,
Who knew fun could always win?

As night comes, they dance and cheer,
Counting stars as they sip a beer.
With the moon as their jolly guide,
They laugh and let the currents ride.

A Taste of the Breeze

With winds that tickle at your nose,
A fruity scent in sunlight glows.
Bananas swing, oh what a chase,
As papayas play hide-and-seek with grace.

The mangoes dance, they jump and twist,
An avocado gives a hearty fist.
Coconuts giggle, rolling down,
While chili peppers wear a crown.

With every bite, a burst of cheer,
Hilarious flavors, oh so dear!
Salsa jams and guacamole dreams,
Tickle your taste with silly themes.

In this land, where joy's a breeze,
Funny fruits bring hearts to ease.
So join the feast, don't be a tease,
Let laughter grow, like sturdy trees.

Mosaic of Fruit

Pineapple hats on teddy bears,
Grapes are dancing, light as air.
Mango jokes that leave you surprised,
Coconut laughter fills the skies.

Limes play hopscotch on the sand,
Bananas slip, oh isn't it grand?
Apples grinning with bright delight,
And cherries blushing in the light.

Strawberry giggles at the beach,
Peach plays hide-and-seek, in reach.
Oranges juggle without a care,
A fruity fest, join if you dare!

In this patchwork of flavor fun,
Every fruit races, on the run.
Nature's jesters, oh what a show,
In this garden, smiles freely grow!

Chasing the Breeze

The wind whispers jokes on a kite,
Balloons waft by, a colorful sight.
Chasing the breeze with laughter in tow,
Tickled by giggles, away they go.

Coconuts grin as they roll along,
Tumbling like misfits in a song.
Waves clap their hands in delight,
Mermaids laugh, under moonlight.

Flip-flops dance on a lively tune,
Sunburned toes, beneath the moon.
Laughter echoes on golden sand,
As friends splash joy, hand in hand.

Catch this breeze, it's fleeting and sweet,
Filled with chuckles, oh what a treat!
The ocean's chuckle, wind's gentle tease,
Join in the frolic, chasing the breeze!

Enchanted Isles

On isles where magic finds its place,
Palm trees gossip with a sunny face.
Paddle boats bob with quirky grace,
While islands giggle in a fun embrace.

Seashells whisper tales of delight,
Waves crack up and dance in the light.
Laughter rides on the ocean's crest,
As crabs in top hats, jest the best.

Turtles bow, taking a brief break,
While seagulls squawk, their silly mistake.
Sand castles wobbly, made with flair,
With giggling kids strewn everywhere.

In this land where mirth's alive,
Frolicking spirits happily thrive.
So grab your hat, join the smiles wide,
On enchanted isles, let joy reside!

Bounty of the Palm

Under palms where the coconuts sway,
Monkeys throw pineapples in play.
Jellybeans tumble, bright in the sun,
As laughter fills the air, oh what fun!

Papayas prance with a wiggly beat,
Limes launch themselves, oh isn't that sweet?
Swaying to rhythms of the bright moon,
In this fruity fiesta, join in soon.

Banana splits race on the sand,
While mangoes offer a friendly hand.
Tropical friends in a wacky race,
Each splash a grin, each laugh a trace.

The bounty's not just of fruit you see,
But of joy and giggles, wild and free.
So come together in this lively charm,
For the heart of the palm is community warm!

Moonlit Marigolds

Under the glow, they dance and sway,
Marigolds giggle, come what may.
A snail in a hat shuffles along,
He hums to the moon, a silly song.

The breeze begins to tickle the leaves,
As fireflies plot their nighttime heaves.
A mouse in a tux takes center stage,
While a dancing frog flips from page to page.

Petals in pajamas, oh what a sight,
They bounce and roll, bursting with light.
A party in blooms, so carefree and bright,
With laughter that sparkles through the night.

In moonlit gardens, the mischief grows,
Between shadowy paths, the fun just flows.
A comedy show of nature's delight,
With marigolds laughing till morning light.

Kaleidoscope of Leaves

Leaves of green with polka dots bold,
They whisper secrets that never get old.
A chameleon pretending to be,
The life of the party, just wait and see.

In the wind, the giggles race and fly,
As branches sway, low and high.
A squirrel in glasses reads the news,
While a sloth does yoga in mismatched shoes.

Colors that clash, a patchwork dance,
Each leaf spins round, caught in a trance.
Funky shapes do a bouncy jig,
As the roots play drums on a coconut fig.

What a sight in this leafy parade,
Where nature's humor is sweetly displayed.
A kaleidoscope of colors and cheer,
Leaves frolic with joy, come gather near.

Coral Garden's Soul

In a sea where colors burst and play,
Corals chuckle in a vibrant array.
An octopus juggles shells with flair,
While a clownfish twirls in the salty air.

Starfish share tales of their ocean days,
As sea turtles glide in a slow ballet.
A playful dolphin jumps high to tease,
While a hermit crab rocks out with ease.

In this garden where watercolors blend,
Every splash brings giggles around each bend.
A parade of bubbles, a splendid sight,
Every wave carries whispers of delight.

Beneath the surface, the laughter ignites,
As creatures gather for fun-filled nights.
A coral reef bursting with life and jest,
In this underwater world, we're truly blessed.

Beyond the Blue Horizon

Where the sky kisses sea with a wink,
Seashells gossip in circles, don't blink.
A crab wearing shades takes a stroll,
While pelicans swoop, stealing the show.

The sun sets low, painting skies bright,
As laughter erupts with the incoming night.
A parrot recites its own silly rhyme,
Making waves dance in the rhythm of time.

Surfboards stacked, ready to ride,
With goofy stickers, they fill up with pride.
Mermaids giggle, playing hide and seek,
While a fish in a tux brings humor unique.

Beyond the horizon, the fun won't cease,
As seabreeze whispers, spreading the peace.
Life's a beach here, with laughter in store,
Where every moment's a chance to adore.

Ballad of the Breeze

A gentle gust plays with my hair,
I chase my hat, it's in mid-air!
The seagulls cackle, they take flight,
As my drink tips over in delight.

The sun is shining, laughter rings,
A hammock sways, my heart it sings!
A crab on the sand gives me a stare,
I wink at it, oh what a pair!

The flip-flops dance, they start to race,
With such charisma, they take their place!
A sudden wave, oh what a splash,
Now I'm soaked, it happened fast!

Wait for the sun, does it always smile?
I drift away, just for a while!
The breeze whispers secrets, quite absurd,
And tickles my toes, oh how I've heard!

Kaleidoscope of Coral

In the water, fish do twirl,
Their scales are bright, they give a whirl!
A turtle munches on a snack,
"Hey buddy, save some for the pack!"

The coral bleaches, oh my, oh me!
A clownfish laughs, says, "Come see!"
The sea anemone gives a wave,
As all the critters misbehave!

A hermit crab puts on a show,
With a fancy shell, it steals the glow!
The starfish giggles, it's in a daze,
"I'm not a star, but in a craze!"

Let's grab our snorkels and take the leap,
Amongst the colors, so bright and deep!
With each stroke, we swim and glide,
In this quirky world, we take such pride!

Citrus Sunsets

As day fades out, the sky's a blend,
A twist of orange, oh what a trend!
Mango slush slips down my chin,
I laugh it off, where to begin?

The palm trees sway, they dance with grace,
I trip on sand, it's quite a race!
A parrot squawks, "You call that cool?"
I retort, "Only if I had a pool!"

The sun dips low, it winks at me,
"Let's have a party, just you and free!"
Lemonade spills, I take a sip,
It's a wild ride, not a boring trip!

A limbo stick, the test of skill,
I barely make it, gives a thrill!
With friends all around, we fade to night,
Under stars, we dance, oh what a sight!

Island Whispers

The palm trees rustle, secrets unsaid,
They giggle softly, never misled!
A coconut falls, it lands with thud,
I dodge it quick, almost in mud!

The waves crash in with a playful roar,
"Join us!" they beckon from the shore!
I take a leap, but woah, what's this?
My belly flop missed, but the splash was bliss!

The crickets chirp a late-night tune,
We dance with shadows under the moon.
A lizard peeks, it's on the run,
"Don't worry mate, this is just for fun!"

With each buoyant laugh, the moments soar,
Island whispers echo, who could ask for more?
A world so silly, where time stands still,
In this outrageous place, we get our fill!

Feast of the Tropics

Coconuts fall with a thud,
Wobbly palms in the warm sun.
Sipping fruity drinks in the mud,
Laughing as the day is won.

Jellyfish dance with grace,
While crabs scuttle quick and sly.
Sunburned noses in the race,
Finding shade with a long sigh.

Mangoes juicy, ripe, and sweet,
Sand between our happy toes.
Biting into heaven's treat,
While seagulls steal our morning prose.

Bananas on a unicycle,
Parrots gossiping with flair.
Each bite brings a new dare,
A feast that tickles the chronicle!

Whispers of the Shore

Waves crash like a giggling child,
Seashells whisper secrets low.
Sunbathers laugh, their sunblock piled,
As wind tosses hair for show.

Beach balls bounce like jolly clowns,
Sandy forts rise with intent.
Seagulls wear their feathered crowns,
Each chirp a playful lament.

A stray flip-flop takes a flight,
Chased by a dog with pure glee.
Laughter echoes, pure delight,
As sand tickles that silly knee.

Underneath the sun's soft rays,
We share jokes that draw a crowd.
In this paradise, we praise,
The fun found in laughter loud!

Canvas of Coastlines

Brush strokes of blue paint the sea,
Palm trees dance in the playful breeze.
A crab in a cocktail hat, oh my!
Painting the coastlines with giggles and sighs.

Pineapple hats? Yes, why not!
Tropical shirts that twirl and spin.
Beach parties that can't be bought,
As waves join our merry din.

Seagulls think they own the show,
While fish peek out with a grin.
Each sunset steals the morning's glow,
Creating laughs from dark to thin.

Silly poses for the camera,
Sandcastle kings raise their crowns.
In this colorful panorama,
We're the circus of seaside towns!

Laughter of Liaisons

Flamingos on roller skates glide,
While monkeys breakdance on the shore.
Every sunset feels bonafide,
Filled with giggles and so much more.

Pineapples hosting a tea party,
Surrounding a table made of sand.
With each sip, they grow quite hearty,
Causing laughter that feels quite grand.

Splashing in with unexpected flair,
Our beach ball flies right through the air.
Tangled hair and silly STARES,
Liaisons float without a care.

Stories shared as the stars come bright,
Matching seaweed hats with pride.
The night wraps us in its light,
As laughter dances with the tide!

A Haven in the Breeze

A parrot jokes, feathers bright,
He steals my drink, what a sight!
I chase him down, we share a laugh,
Splashing juice on my other half.

In hammocks sway, we take our ease,
Between two palms, a gentle tease.
The coconut falls, a thud with glee,
It rolls away, setting us free!

With sand that sticks, we're one big mess,
The sun keeps shining, we must confess.
A world of mischief, we can't resist,
And how we giggle at each twist!

A breeze that tickles, a breeze that jokes,
We dance and stumble like silly folks.
In this bright land, so wild and free,
We find our joy, just you and me.

Pineapple Sunsets

The sun dips low, a fruity ball,
Bikini-clad, I trip and fall.
A pineapple hat? What a sight!
I wear it proud, oh what delight!

With shades askew, I stroll the shore,
Stumbling over, I wish for more.
A seagull snickers, swoops in close,
It snags my snack, that feathered ghost!

A sunset's glow, a peachy hue,
The laughter echoes, I join the crew.
As waves crash loud, we sing along,
To silly tunes and a playful song.

With sandy toes and salty hair,
We dance like nobody is there.
In this bright glow, we find our laughs,
Who knew a fruit could spark such gaffs?

Waves of Laughter

The ocean calls, with a bubbling cheer,
We chase the waves, with no fear.
A splash, a giggle, a race to the shore,
Who knew that water could hold so much lore?

A crab scuttles by, all shiny and red,
I try to catch it, but bump my head.
As friends all chuckle, I strike a pose,
With sandy bums and friendly woes.

The seagulls squawk, they join the spree,
Diving for fries, oh what glee!
We roll in the surf, the fun never ends,
In this sea-filled life, we're all best friends.

With each wave's crash, we share our dreams,
Through laughter and joy, life bursts at the seams.
In a sandy playground, we make our mark,
Chasing sunsets 'til it's completely dark.

The Call of the Sand

Here on the shore, the grains unite,
A dance of joy, a spark of light.
I trip on my towel, a perfect faceplant,
In a sea of giggles, I truly can't chant.

The kids build castles, with moats and towers,
They challenge me, their laughter empowers.
But when the tide comes in with a swoosh,
Those towers tumble, a watery push!

A game of beachball, we all take a stand,
But balls go flying, oh isn't that grand?
A kick to the left, then a swerve to the right,
We're rolling on laughing from morning to night.

As dusk descends, we watch it unfold,
Each laugh a treasure, more precious than gold.
With stories to tell, and memories to weave,
In this sunny paradise, it's hard to believe.

Secrets of the Mangroves

In the mangroves, crabs dance around,
With tiny top hats, they leap off the ground.
Fish in tuxedos swim by, oh so spry,
While a parrot mimics a karaoke guy.

Coconuts gossip about the breeze's tales,
As lizards run off, their colorful scales.
A monkey swings with a laugh and a yell,
And drops a banana, oh, what a smell!

The mud-sticky shoes make a squishy sound,
As everyone's feet get stuck to the ground.
An owl in a tree, reading a book,
Says, "I thought this was a quiet nook!"

But in the shadowed roots, laughter will rise,
With silly creatures in silly disguises.
Join the fun, let your heart take a chance,
In these mangrove secrets, it's a wild dance!

Serene Lagoon Echoes

In the lagoon where the turtles play,
They have tea parties at the end of the day.
The frogs croak songs in a funny duet,
While fish wear sunglasses, lookin' quite set.

The palm trees sway, dancing to a tune,
While a crab conducts under the light of the moon.
A floating duck with a floral crown,
Insists it's king of this watery town.

Echoes of giggles linger in the air,
As a snail offers rides, though it's quite rare.
"Hop on my shell, we're off on a spree!"
Squeaks a swift gecko, "Let's see what we see!"

But as dusk fills the lagoon with its grace,
The critters chuckle, and join in the race.
With laughter as currency, love as the key,
Their echoing joy carries over the sea!

Beneath the Palms

Beneath the palms, where the shadows play,
A turtle in shades claims it's his day.
The sunbather cockroach is working on tan,
While a crab in a chair yells, "I'm your man!"

Parrots are gossiping by the coconut stand,
Trading whispers like they are in a band.
With cocktails of nectar, they toast to the day,
While a lazy old sloth just sleeps all the way.

The wind tells jokes through the rustling fronds,
While lizards sit sipping their magical ponds.
A party's in session, but only for fun,
Underneath the palms, where the laughter's begun.

So join in the mirth, grab a fruit from the tree,
As laughter spreads wide, wild, and carefree.
Life under the palms is a giggly delight,
Where day turns to night in a breeze of sheer light!

Whispering Waves

Whispers from waves tease the sandy shore,
As a crab throws a dance, then shuffles for more.
The gulls wear hats, oh, such a sight,
Squawking "Let's party! We'll dance through the night!"

The fishes in gowns glide with elegant flair,
While starfish cheer with their wild, wiggly air.
A dolphin zooms in, performing a trick,
And splashes the crowd with a splashy flick!

With each funny tumble, a giggle erupts,
As sea turtles watch, and join in the cups.
"Let's make a toast!" the seaweed shouts loud,
For fun in the sun makes a joyful crowd!

So let the waves whisper their sweet, silly dreams,
In the laughter of sea life, nothing's as it seems.
Join the playful spirits, let happiness flow,
In a seaside frolic where giggles will grow!

www.ingramcontent.com/pod-product-compliance
Lightning Source LLC
Chambersburg PA
CBHW072218070526
44585CB00015B/1394